Kids Travel & Learn

New York City

Dear Parents,
We hope you have a great visit in New York City
and that you and your children enjoy this book!
The Kids Travel & Learn series is developed to be a rich hands-on educational experience for children of elementary school age. It is suitable for older children to work through independently while younger children are likely to need some help to get the most out of the book.
The Kids Travel and Learn series is developed by Leo Kids LLC.
Please visit our website at www.leokidstravel.com for more information, to provide feedback, or to purchase additional books. Thank you!
Sincerely,
Annika & Vanessa

ISBN: 1449916317

Who am I?

My name is .... and I am .... years old.

My home town is ....

I am in .... grade at .... school.

This is my .... trip to New York City.

I am traveling to NYC with ....

I came to NYC by: (Circle one of the images below)

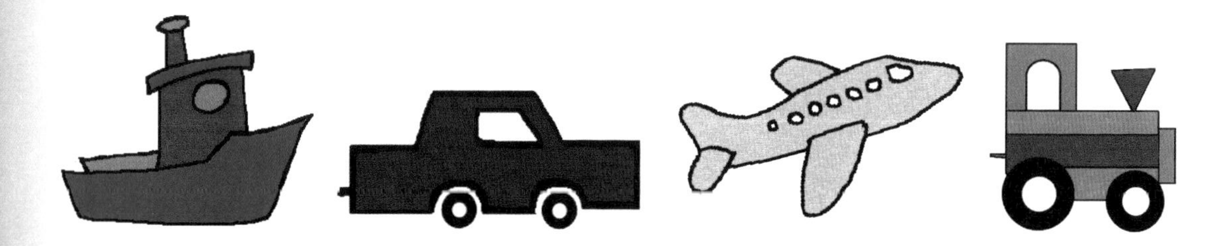

I arrived in NYC on .... and

leave to go home on ....

This means, I will be in NYC for .... days.

Mark on the clocks below what time you arrived and what time you will leave.

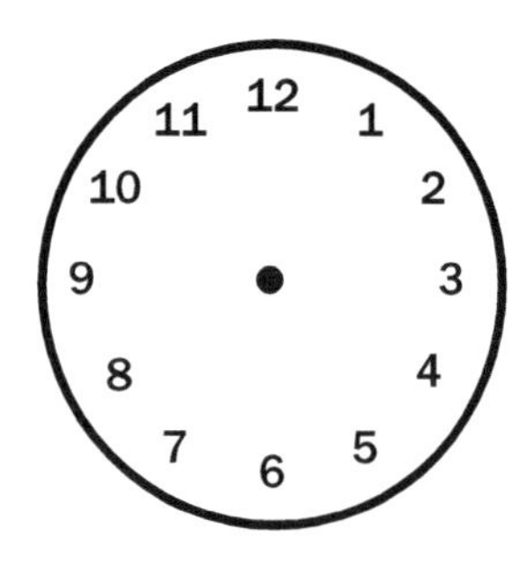

Arrival Time

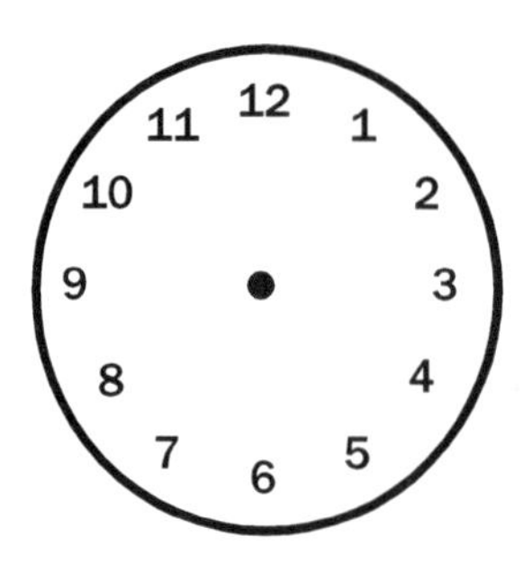

Departure Time

Did you notice we used NYC instead of New York City? This is called an acronym. Can you spot some more acronyms around NYC?

In NYC, I will be staying at ....

My favorite part about traveling is ....

My least favorite part about traveling is ....

I am excited to go to .... in NYC.

The most important thing I packed is my ....

Here I am traveling to NYC:

I am .... feet .... inches tall.

I have .... colored hair.

I have .... colored eyes.

My favorite color is ....

The Big Apple is a nickname for NYC. Keep an eye out for the Big Apple symbol around town. Use Tally Marks to count how many times you see it ....

Where in the world am I?

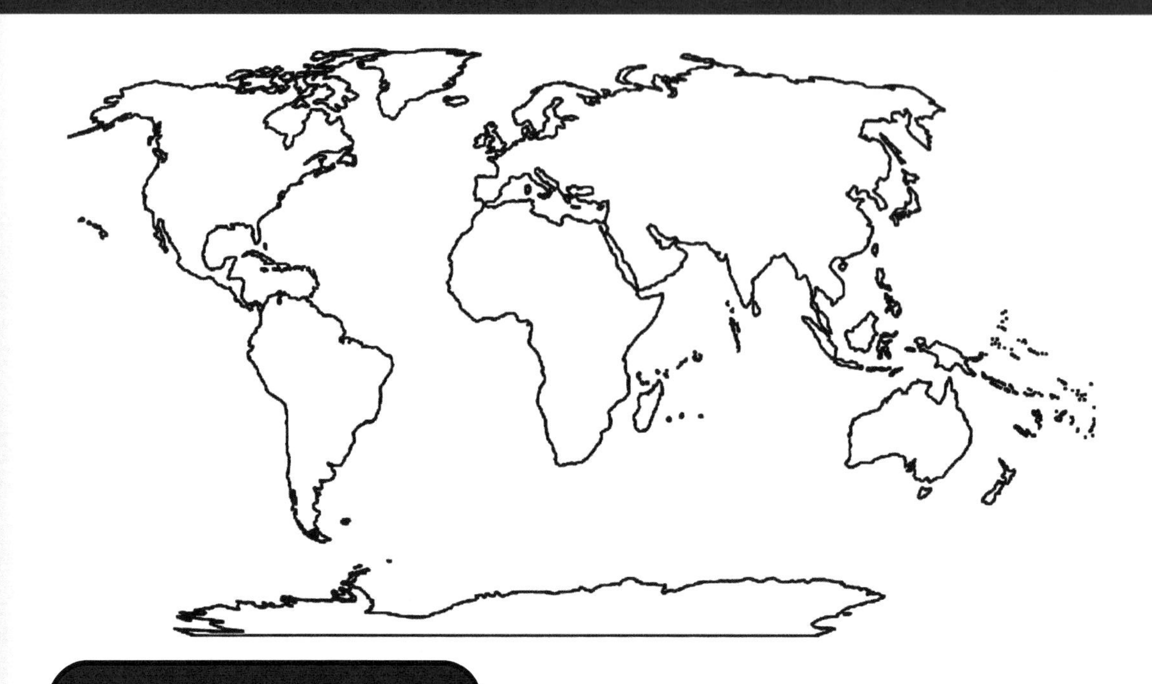

The United States of America belongs to the continent of North America. Color in the North American continent on the map. Next, try to name the other continents.

NYC is located in the state of New York, on the east coast of the United States. Color it on the map as well as any other states you have been to.

New York City is located in a natural, protected harbor where the Hudson River meets the Atlantic Ocean. This harbor has been critical to NYC's growth, as harbors are very important to a city's ability to trade with other cities and countries.

If you look up some big cities around the world on a map, you will notice that many of them have very good harbors!

Draw columns on the chart to show how many continents, countries, states and big cities you have visited.

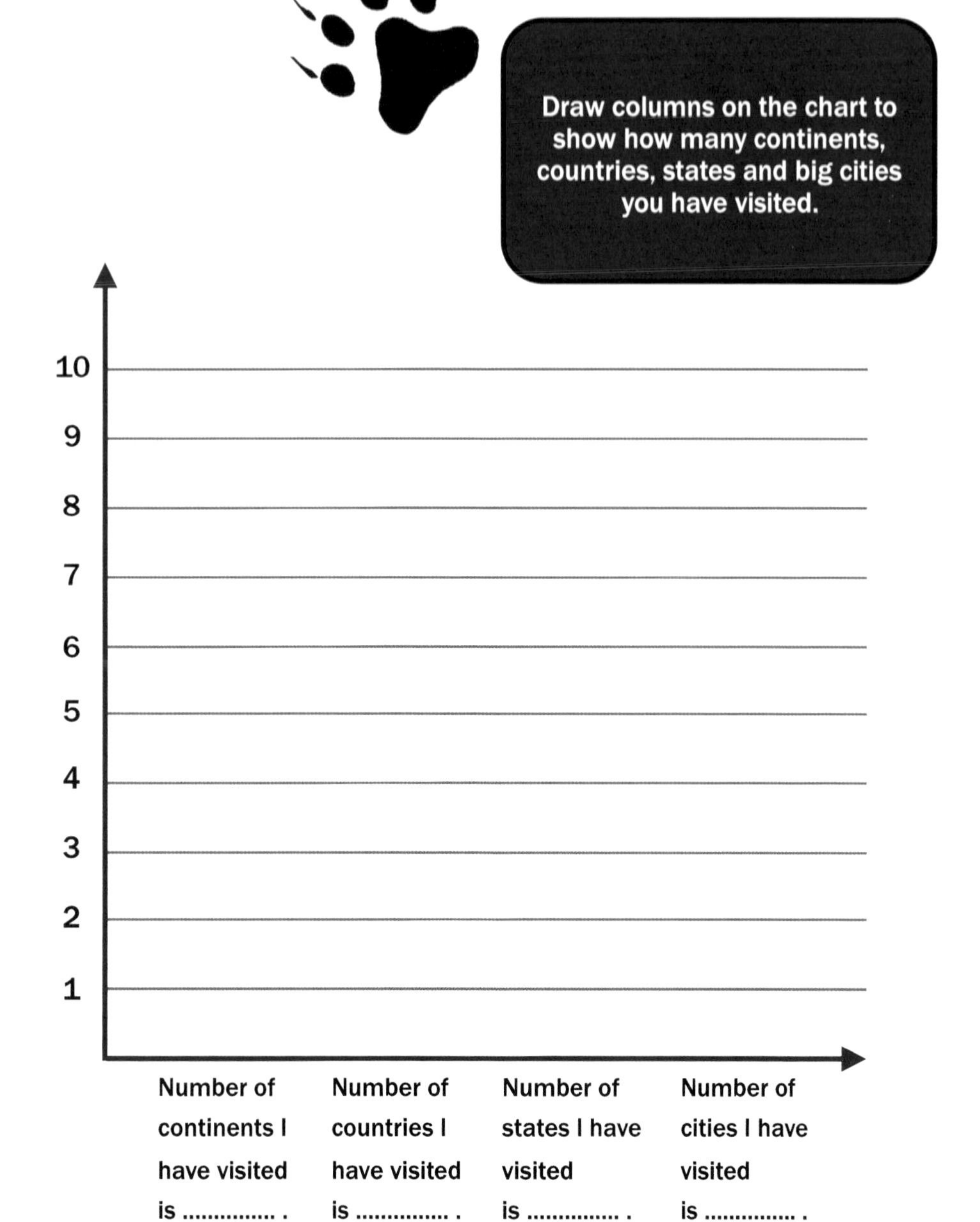

Who's been here before?

A LONG TIME AGO — Lenape Indians live in the area that is now NYC. In their language, Manhattan means "Island of the Hills." They live off hunting, fishing and farming.

1524 — Giovanni Di Verrazano is the first European to sail into New York Harbor.

1609 — Henry Hudson reaches Manhattan on his exploratory voyage.

1613 — The first Europeans settle in Lower Manhattan. The Dutch use the area as a base for fur trading.

1626 — The Dutch buy Manhattan from the Indians. Some say the price was $65. The settlement at the tip of Manhattan is named New Amsterdam.

1790 — The capital of the US is moved to Philadelphia.

1825 — The Erie Canal opens allowing the Port of New York to reach the Great Lakes via the Hudson River.

1857 — Central Park landscaping commences.

1861 - 1865 — The Civil War.

1886 — The Statue of Liberty is raised.

1667

Peter Stuyvesant becomes the last Dutch Director-General of New Amsterdam.

1664

The English conquer New Amsterdam. They change the name to New York.

1700

The Lenape population is down to about 200 due to wars, epidemics and displacement.

1775 - 1783

The Revolutionary war.

1789

George Washington is inaugurated as President of the United States in Federal Hall on Wall Street. New York City is the capital of the U.S.

Spot the *ten* differences between the picture on the left and the picture on the right.

1892

The Ellis Island Immigration Station is opened.

1898

Manhattan, the Bronx, Brooklyn, Queens and Staten Island become New York City.

1914 - 1918

The First World War.

1931

The Empire State Building is completed.

1939 - 1945

The Second World War.

How did NYC become NYC anyway?

LEO QUIZ

1. Using the timeline on the previous page, work out how many years passed between each of these events:

   a. The first Europeans settling in Lower Manhattan AND George Washington being inaugurated as President? ....

   b. Central Park landscaping commencement AND Ellis Island opening? ....

   c. The end of the Revolutionary War AND the start of the Civil War? ....

2. Like New York, many places in the U.S. are named after places in the immigrant's home countries. List some places with "New" in it close to where you live:

   .... , ... , ...

3. What has been named after the following people in New York history?

   a. Peter **Stuyvesant**

      i. Garden ii. Square iii. Sidewalk

   b. Giovanni da **Verrazano**

      i. Building ii. Bridge iii. Gate

   c. Henry **Hudson**

      i. River ii. Parkway iii. Both

Answers: 1. a. 176, b. 35, c. 78. 3. a. ii, b. ii, c. iii.

4. Complete the rhymes in the phrases below!

a. On Henry Hudson's exploratory .... ,
he reached Manhattan, which is now so hip.

b. Once in this area, the Lenape Indians would .... ,
from which they could certainly serve you a tasty dish!

c. The Lenape had both fishing and hunting skills,
in their language Manhattan means "Island of
the ...."

d. In 1626 the Indians sold Manhattan to the ....
It is said they did not pay very much.

e. 1789 was the year of George Washington's ....
New York City was then the capital of this great nation.

f. In 1886 the Statue of Liberty was .... ,
everyone watching was truly amazed.

g. Ellis Island is a very interesting location,
is has been a funnel for much ....

h. The Bronx, Brooklyn, Manhattan, Queens and Staten Island
are the boroughs .... ,
since 1898, as New York City, together they strive.

Answers: a. trip, b. fish, c. hills, d. Dutch, e. inauguration, f. raised, g. immigration, h. five.

What makes up New York City?

New York City is the most *densely populated* city in the United States. Densely populated means that a lot of people live very close to each other in a small space!

Most of NYC is built on three islands - Manhattan, Staten Island, and the western part of Long Island.

NYC is divided into five *boroughs*. Boroughs are different parts of the city. These are the Bronx, Brooklyn, Manhattan, Queens, and Staten Island.

There is also a lot of water running through, and surrounding, New York City: the Hudson River, East River, Harlem River, Long Island Sound and the Atlantic Ocean.

NYC has its own government with an *elected* Mayor at the top of its Executive branch. Elected means the Mayor is chosen by the people living in NYC. The NYC Council, with 51 members, has the *legislative* power in the city. Legislative means they write the laws.

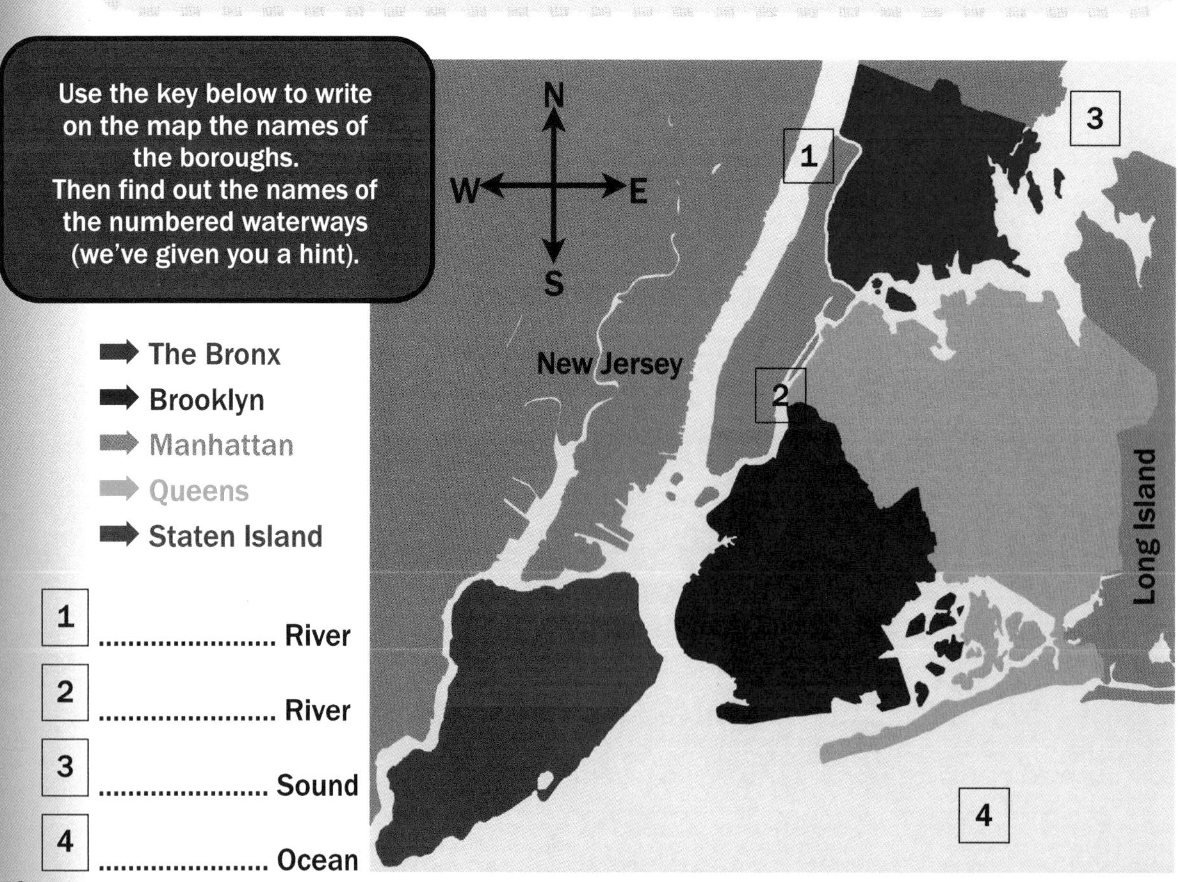

Answers: 1-Hudson, 2-East, 3-Long Island, 4-Atlantic.

Borough	Size (Sq. miles)	Population*
The Bronx	42	1,373,659
Brooklyn	71	2,528,050
Manhattan	23	1,620,867
Queens	110	2,270,338
Staten Island	58	481,613
Total NYC:		

*Based on 2007 CENSUS Bureau estimates.
A *census* is a process to count the people living in an area.

This table shows the size and population of the boroughs of NYC. If you are a Math Whiz, try to calculate the total size and population on your own!

LEO QUIZ

1. Using the table which is the largest borough in size in NYC?

   a. Queens b. Brooklyn c. Manhattan

2. Which is the smallest borough in NYC?

   a. Staten Island b. The Bronx c. Manhattan

3. Where do most people live?

   a. The Bronx b. Queens c. Brooklyn

4. Which boroughs are on the island called "Long Island"?

   a. Manhattan/The Bronx b. Brooklyn/Queens

   c. Staten Island/Brooklyn

5. What river runs just West of Queens and Brooklyn?

   a. The East River b. Harlem River c. Hudson River

6. Can you go by boat from New York to Chicago?

   a. I don't know b. Yes c. No

Can you find out who is the current Mayor of New York City?

Answers: 1-a, 2-c, 3-c, 4-b, 5-a, 6-b.

Where in NYC am I?

In Manhattan most of the streets in the North-South direction are called Avenues, and most of the Streets that run East-West are called Streets. As you are getting to know your way around, it is very helpful that many of these are also named by numbers! First Avenue is far East on Manhattan and Fifth Avenue pretty much runs down the middle. Street names start with *East* if they are East of Fifth Avenue and *West* if they are West of Fifth Avenue. When you are walking around the city it is good to know that if you walk north or south for twenty blocks, that is about one mile.

Find your way through the maze by bicycle to the Empire State Building. Don't forget to take a bite out of the Big Apple along the way.

1. Let's help Leo get around town! Following a subway map, write down the train lines he needs to take and stations he needs to change at.

   a. Leo has just arrived in NYC and wants to get from JFK Airport to his hotel in Times Square: .... , ...

   b. After a good night's sleep, Leo is ready to go to the Metropolitan Museum of Art: .... , ...

   c. After finding the Pyramids (did you?), Leo is ready to go to the Statue of Liberty: .... , ... , ...

   d. The following morning Leo leaves his hotel in Times Square and travels out to the Bronx Zoo: .... , ...

2. Now use a map to help you answer these questions:

   a. Name the Avenue between 3rd Ave & Park Ave? ....

   b. What is another name for 6th Ave? ....

   c. Name the Avenues along Central Park .... , ...

One of the best ways to get around New York City is to use Public Transportation. In NYC the MTA (Metropolitan Transportation Authority) can get you almost anywhere you need to go. There are subways and buses to get you - and about five million other people each day - around the city. You can also take a taxi - or a *cab* as most New Yorkers would say. There are over ten thousand (10,000) yellow cabs in NYC so you'll see lots of them!
Without public transportation NYC would not be the city it is today - imagine the traffic jams, pollution and noise from all the cars if everyone was driving themselves around town!

What can I eat here?

New York City has lots of great restaurants and delicious foods! There are more than 20,000 restaurants in NYC! That means that if you go to a new restaurant every day it would take you over 50 years to visit all of them! At that point many of them are probably not there any longer but new ones will have opened.

In NYC you can eat almost any type of food you like! One great thing about that is that you are going to find lots of delicious healthy food choices in NYC. Also, it's exciting to try foods from all over the world!

NYC is also known for some special foods like bagels, New York style pizza, steaks, hotdogs, deli sandwiches and there is, of course, plenty of fine dining! Many of the best chefs in the world work in NYC.

Continue the patterns below on some of these favorite NYC food items.

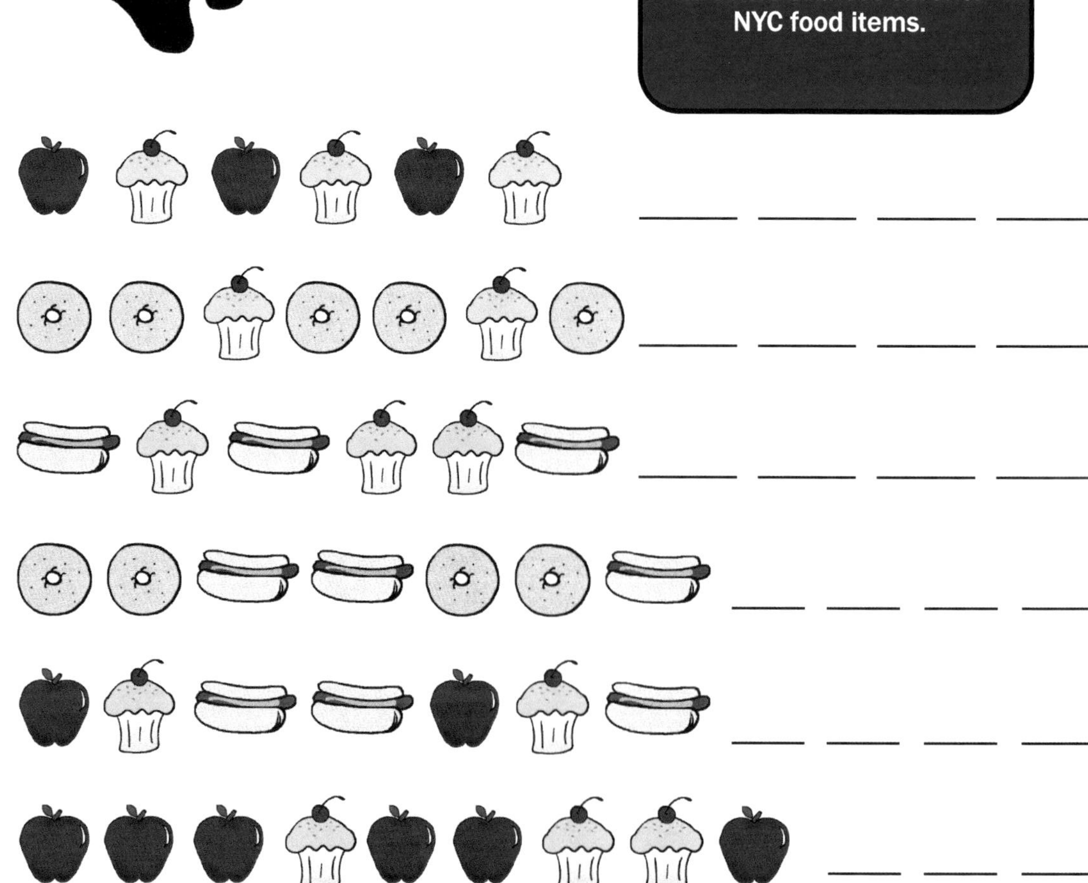

LEO QUIZ

1. On the pizza below circle the slice you'd eat first if you love pepperoni!
2. Now, circle the slice you'd eat if you don't like pepperoni.
3. On the pizza on the right draw on the toppings you would choose for your own pizza. Some ideas are pictured.
4. How many pieces are each pizza divided into? ....

5. If you were to divide this pizza into quarters how many slices would be in each quarter? ....
6. If you ate two slices of pizza, how many slices would be left? ....
7. What fraction of the pizza would four slices be? ....

What lives & grows here?

There is one species of rat in New York City - the Norway rat.
As in many cities, NYC has a lot of rats running around.
When rats are scared they fluff up their fur to look bigger.
Norway rats, or Brown rats, have acute hearing, but poor vision.
They are *nocturnal*, which means they are mostly awake at night.
They are also good diggers and swimmers and will eat pretty much anything - including lots of trash!

**Color in the Rat and take note of its distinguishing features.
Keep a look out for rats in NYC, especially in the subway.**

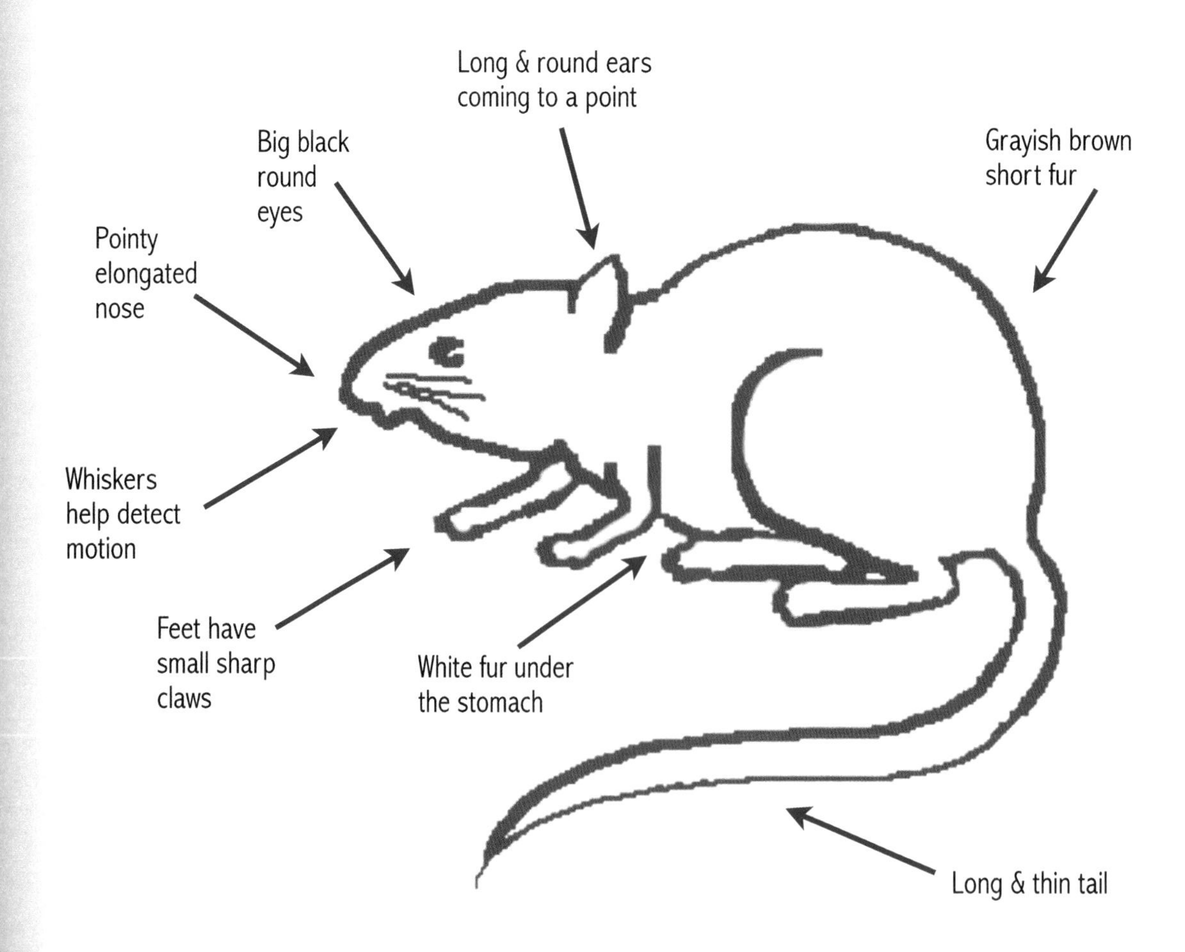

The most common tree in Central Park is the American Elm. The latin name is *Ulmus Americana*.

The American Elm is a *deciduous* tree, which means its leaves fall off seasonally. It is the largest elm in the United States and can grow to over 115 feet tall and 10 feet in diameter. It can live for several hundred years and is very hardy.

Dutch elm disease is a very big problem for American Elms all over the country. It is a fungal disease which has killed many old American Elms but not all of them. Some of the old American Elms in Central Park have been protected from this disease because they are fairly isolated from other Elm trees.

See if you can find an elm tree and pick up a leaf off the ground. Study the interesting patterns in the veins of the leaf.

All the animals listed below can be found in NYC. Circle them in the word search.

E	P	S	Q	U	I	R	R	E	L
K	L	O	C	A	S	R	R	G	S
W	O	M	D	S	P	A	O	D	P
O	P	R	A	C	A	D	F	B	I
R	A	B	D	O	R	B	F	O	G
C	R	O	R	G	R	R	P	C	E
C	O	C	K	R	O	A	C	H	O
S	B	I	S	G	W	H	A	F	N
H	I	B	E	R	A	T	T	I	O
K	N	U	M	P	I	H	C	A	B

Rat
Dog
Crow
Cat
Bass
Elm
Carp

Sparrow
Pigeon
Cockroach
Robin
Chipmunk
Squirrel
Frog

Where is the Statue of Liberty from?

The Statue of Liberty is a symbol of freedom and democracy. It was given to the United States by France. It was planned to be a centennial gift from France to the United States in 1876, to commemorate the 100 years that had passed since the American Declaration of Independence, however, it took more time than expected to complete and was raised on Ellis Island in 1886. Twelve million (12,000,000) immigrants entered the United States through Ellis Island!

The statue is covered with copper and the torch is covered with sheets of 24 karat gold. The copper is now green because of oxidation, which is a natural chemical process in copper. The seven rays on the Statue's crown symbolize each of the seven continents.

The Statue of Liberty holds a torch in her right hand and a tablet in her left. The tablet is inscribed with "July IV MDCCLXXVI", which means July 4, 1776. This is another way of writing numbers, called Roman numerals. The numbers we use (1, 2, 3, and so on) are called Arabic numbers.

4	LXII
8	CCL
20	MMLII
35	CLXXX
55	XCIV
62	CVIII
94	MCMLXXXVI
108	XXXV
180	IV
250	XX
1986	LV
2052	VIII

Roman		Arabic
I	=	1
V	=	5
X	=	10
L	=	50
C	=	100
D	=	500
M	=	1,000

Use the key to help you connect the Arabic numbers to the Roman numerals. Hint: 40 = XL *not* XXXX

How big is Central Park anyway?

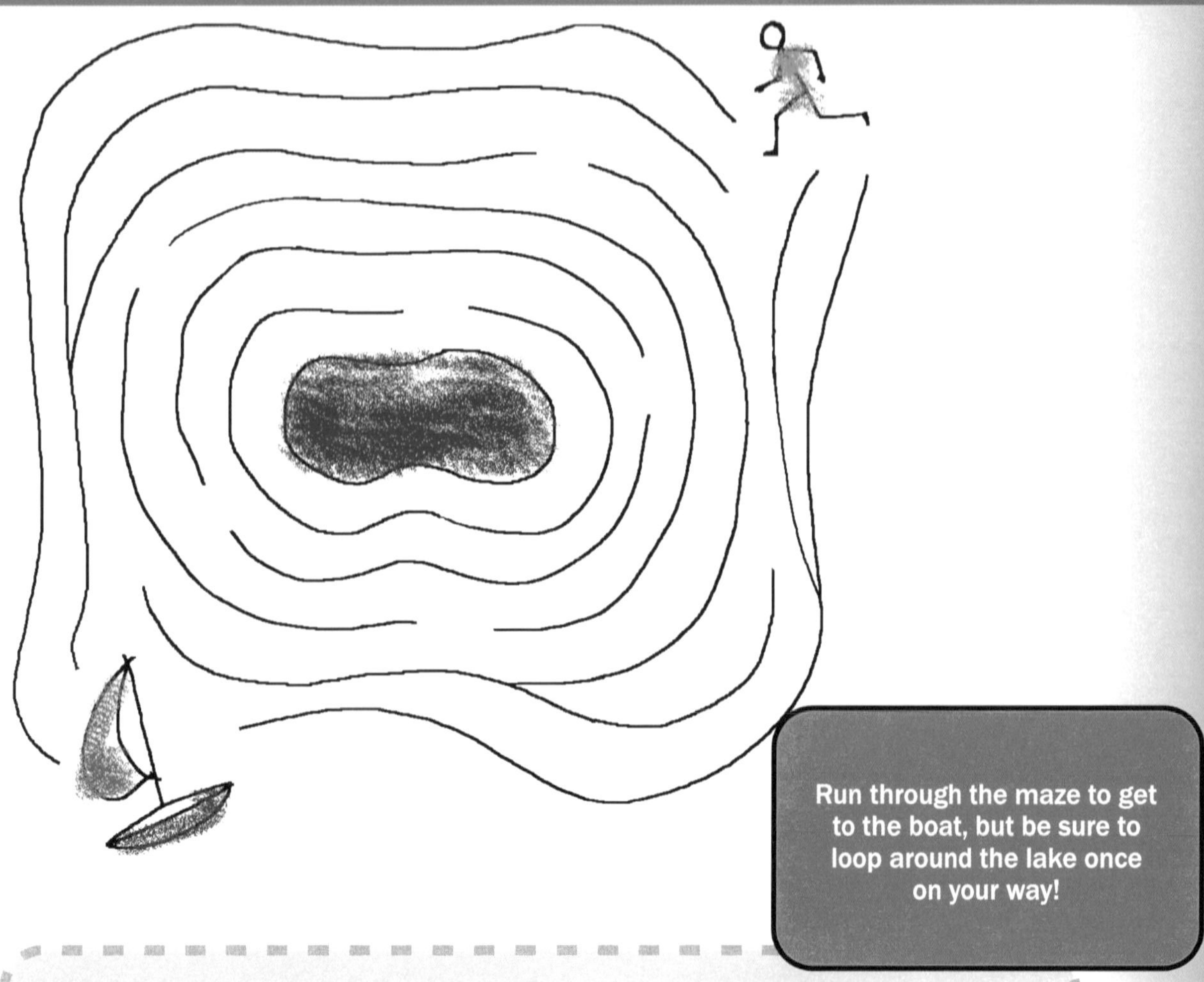

Run through the maze to get to the boat, but be sure to loop around the lake once on your way!

Central Park is a large park - over one square mile - in the center of Manhattan. About 25 million people visit Central Park every year.
The park is mostly *landscaped*, even though many areas look like they are growing wild. Landscaped means that the area has been planned and built to look a certain way.
Central Park has lots of fun activities for both New Yorkers and visitors. Depending on the season, some of the fun things you can do and visit in Central Park include ice skating rinks, swimming pool, row boats on the lake, walking tracks, climbing, rollerblading, Central Park Zoo, horse-drawn carriages and lots of playgrounds. Belvedere Castle is also a very cool place to visit! There are lots of performances in Central Park. You can just walk around and run into street performers, or look up the schedule for public theatre and musical shows and concerts, or even buy tickets to a marionette show at the Swedish Cottage.

How tall is the Empire State Building?

LEO QUIZ

Pick-up a brochure at the Empire State Building to help you answer the following questions:

1. How many elevators are in the Empire State Building (or ESB)?

   a. 25 b. 73 c. 104

2. How many floors are in the ESB?

   a. 55 b. 82 c. 103

3. What year did construction of the ESB start?

   a. 1930 b. 1936 c. 1955

4. What is the height of the ESB?

   a. 550 ft b. 1,101 ft c. 1,454 ft

5. How many windows in the ESB?

   a. 4,200 b. 6,500 c. 10,200

6. How many man-hours went into building the ESB?

   a. 250,000 b. 7,000,000

   c. 50,000,000

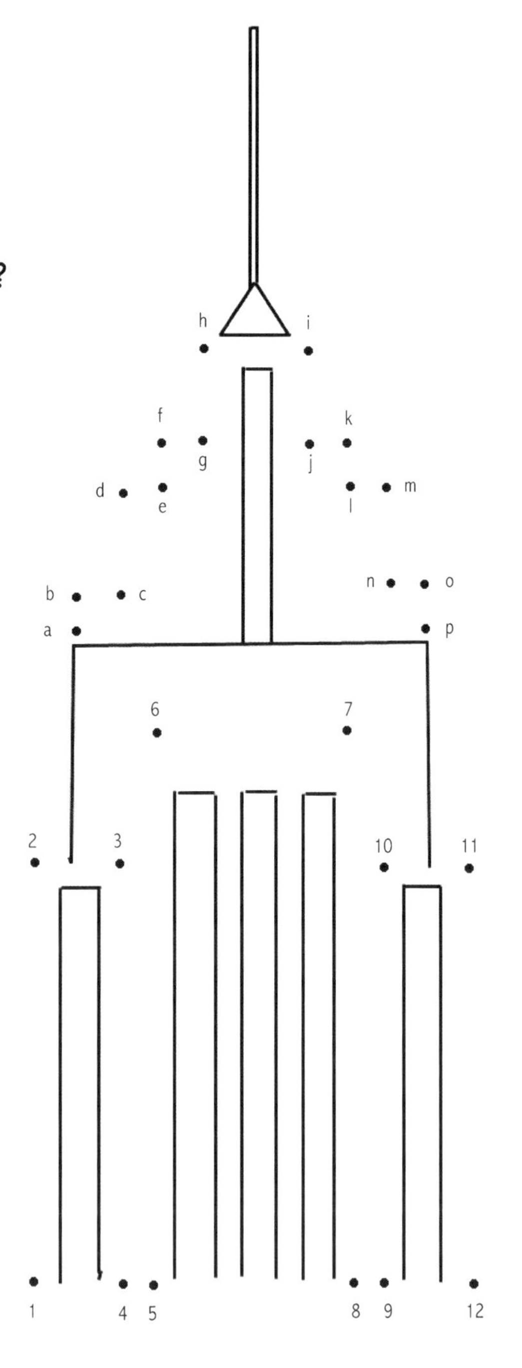

Connect the dots on the Empire State Building opposite. First try the numbers, then the letters.

Answers: 1-b, 2-c, 3-a, 4-c, 5-b, 6-b.

Is Times Square really square?

Times Square was named after the famous newspaper *The New York Times* built their new headquarters in the square in 1904.
Times Square is known as the heart of the theatre district. Lots of people visit Times Square, and many see shows in the area every day. Times Square is also known for all its billboards that keep the square well lit at night!
On New Year's Eve each year about half a million (500,000) people come to see the ball drop in Times Square to ring in the New Year. This was done for the first time in 1907.

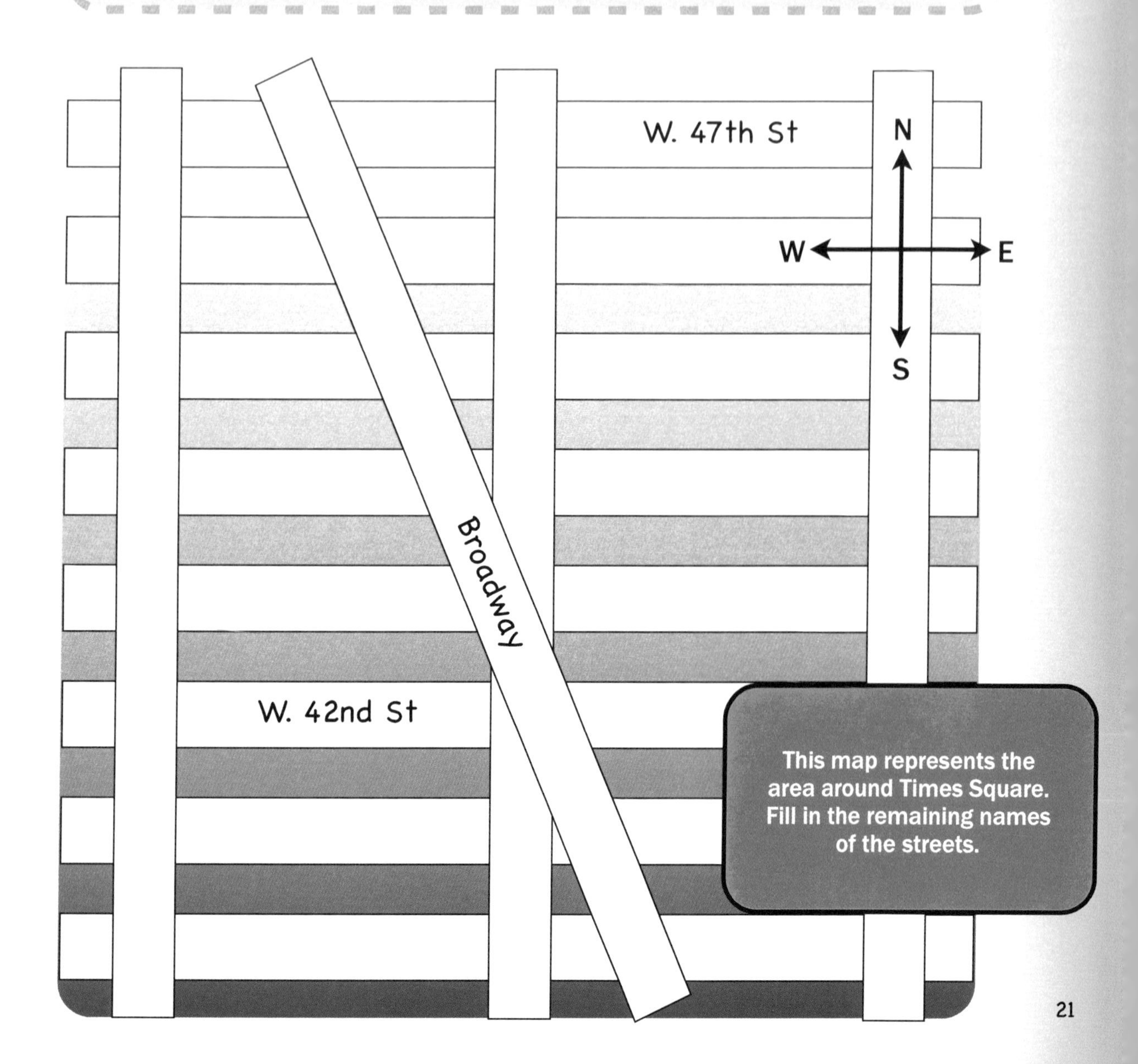

What sports do they like here?

New Yorkers love their sports and there are many teams to follow. NYC has teams in all of the major professional leagues - NFL, NHL, NBA and the two MLB divisions - the American League and National League. NYC also hosts many other big sporting events, such as the New York Marathon and the US Open in tennis.

A really crazy time in NYC for sports fans is when there is a "Subway Series." That is when the baseball World Series is played between two New York City teams. That has happened fourteen times so far - and it has pretty much everyone in the city rooting for one of the teams!

Ticker-tape parades are for special occasions - and have been known to be held for NYC sports teams when they win a championship!

See if you can connect the correct team with the right sport and stadium.
Hint: Several teams can be connected to the same sport/stadium.

What's fun in NYC?

Color in the shape next to the NYC Highlights. Choose the category according to what you have seen & done in NYC.

	Favorite!	Just did it!	Next time!	Not my thing
American Girl Place				
American Museum of Natural History				
Broadway Show				
Bronx Zoo				
Central Park				
Chinatown				
Coney Island				
Empire State Building				
FAO Schwarz				
Intrepid Sea-Air-Space Museum				
Madame Tussauds Wax Museum				
Metropolitan Museum of Art				
National Museum of American Indians				
New York Aquarium				
New York City Fire Museum				
New York City Police Museum				
Restaurant				
South Street Seaport				
Sports Event				
Statue of Liberty				
Times Square				
Wall Street				

What did I do in NYC?

Write a story about your visit to New York City. Try to include as many of these places and words as you can on one page: Grand Central Station, Big Apple, New York Times, skyscraper, subway, sidewalk, noise, city, hotel. Ask someone for more paper if you run out of space!

Go back & check your work. As you do, count how many of Leo's Paws you see throughout the book. I count .... Paws.